FABU...

PARTY

PIECES

Scrumptious hot and cold finger
food for entertaining a crowd.

MURDOCH BOOKS®

Sydney • London • Vancouver • New York

Easy entertaining

Making light work of entertaining is something you may think only the professionals can do. Not so. However modest your culinary skills, you can still put on a good spread and make your friends feel a part of something special. With the right mix of guests, the right food (tailored to suit your capabilities) and the right attitude of mind, you can't go far wrong. Planning ahead is the sure-fire way to success.

All parties, whether large or small, call for good organisation. Draw up a list of what you plan to cook and all the items you will need to go out and buy. Prepare a blow-by-blow timetable covering the two days or so before the party. Itemise the labour-intensive work such as the shopping (food, drinks, glasses and tableware) and the initial stages of cooking that can be dealt with at a reasonable, anxiety-free pace. That way you know that, should something go wrong, you'll have time to rectify the problem.

Frantic last-minute shopping results in the unnecessary expense of your precious time, energy and hard-earned cash. Frantic last-minute cooking is simply rife with the possibility of being heavy-handed with the pastry, burning the sauce or letting the milk boil over.

The day of the cocktail party, pre-theatre drinks, office farewell – or whatever the occasion is that you're busy organising – should be left clear for the final stages of the food preparation and cooking, laying the table, flower arranging and chilling the drinks. The only shopping you should do is for fresh vegetables, fruit, salad ingredients and flowers.

This book specifically deals with finger food for parties of all sizes. Portable food is the name of the game. This is no place for floppy open sandwiches doomed to dispense their toppings onto the carpet, nor for overlarge tarts with runny fillings that will stain someone's favourite silk dress.

When your guests are standing up with a glass in one hand and a handbag/child/sheaf of papers to worry about, too, they need compact food that can be easily popped into their mouths with no crumbs, no spills and definitely no plate, knife and fork.

The do-ahead factor

The recipes featured here have been chosen for their ease of preparation and with the 'do-ahead' factor firmly in mind. Many items such as bread and pastry cases, sauces, fillings and toppings can often be made a day or two before they are required. Marinades do a lot of the work for you, flavouring and tenderising meat, chicken, seafood and fruit overnight or for several hours during the

---

Clockwise from top: Prawn Toast, Steamed Dim Sims, Spring Rolls (all recipes on page 52).

day, leaving you free to attend to other matters. Thread the pieces of food on skewers on the day and cook them for a few minutes just before serving. They'll taste as though you have had to put in a lot more work than that!

And if you are really pressed for time, don't be afraid to 'dress up' ready-made items from delicatessens. Jars of pesto, olive paste and tahini are indispensable to have on hand in the pantry, and vol-au-vent cases, different types of bread and various types of pastry – shortcrust, filo, puff – can be kept for several weeks in the freezer and pressed into service at short notice.

The storecupboard

A well-stocked larder is definitely one of the ways to streamline the entertaining process, so take a long, hard look at yours and stock up on those essential items such as tomato paste, tins of tomatoes, jars of preserved fruits, spicy sauces, mayonnaise and a good range of oils and vinegars infused with herbs that will do most of the work for you in turning something run-of-the-mill into something special.

Celebration Punch

Here is an ideal punch to serve on a special occasion. Add the icy cold champagne just before serving. It will not be necessary to add ice to this punch. The quantities given are sufficient for 12 people. Double the ingredients for a larger gathering.

1 x 250 g punnet strawberries
2 tablespoons icing sugar
180 mL brandy
180 mL Cointreau
2 x 750 mL bottles champagne

1 Hull strawberries and halve if large, place in a punch bowl. Sprinkle fruit with the icing sugar.
2 Add brandy and Cointreau, stir lightly to combine. Stand the punch, covered, in the refrigerator for several hours.
3 To serve, pour in the chilled champagne.

Variety

It always pays to serve some hot items of food alongside the cold, even during the warmest weather. People like variety and you should consider a balance of flavours (mild to spicy), textures (smooth to crunchy) and, of course, the look of the food. If everything is green and brown, that will hardly excite the tastebuds. Put on a colourful spread. Aim to serve six to eight different items for about 20 people. Presentation is important, too. Pretty serving platters and attractive (but also sturdy) glassware help to create the right mood.

Easy drinks

When it comes to the drinks, pre-planning is important. Many liquor shops will supply the wine and soft drinks you require on a sale or return basis, and many also hire out glassware and can provide drinks waiters, if needed, all as part of the 'package'.

Tell the supplier how many people you are expecting, what kind of age groups you are catering for and the sort of food you plan to serve, and let them estimate what you will need. If you prefer to do all this for yourself, bear in mind that one 750 mL bottle of wine holds six glasses and each 750 mL bottle of spirits holds 25-30 shots. Over a couple of hours, a moderate drinker will consume half a bottle of wine. If the occasion is informal and you are serving mainly beer, allow three drinks per person. If the event is to last three or four hours, adjust the amounts accordingly. But make sure you keep the food and drink coming. Always have plenty of soft drinks and mineral water available, particularly if there are teenagers and children attending the party. Also, if the weather is hot, the consumption of cold, light drinks will escalate and your guests will wilt if there is not plenty to hand. If the function is being held outdoors – on a boat or at the beach, for instance – this is even more important. Freshly made vegetable and fruit juices are always appreciated. Use your blender and a squeezer attachment to your food processor. The homemade results are always worth the effort.

If you're serving a fruity punch, chill it well with lots of large

Pimm's Punch

Have all the ingredients well chilled and add the orange juice and champagne just before serving time. The quantities given are sufficient for 12-16 people. Serve in highball glasses.

ice
375 mL Pimm's No 2
375 mL Southern
  Comfort
180 mL sweet
  vermouth
180 mL light rum
375 mL orange juice
1 x 750 mL bottle
  champagne
fresh fruit
orange and lemon slices

1 Place ice in punch bowl. Add Pimm's, Southern Comfort, vermouth and rum; stir to mix.
2 Pour in orange juice and champagne. Add fresh fruits and orange and lemon slices. Serve at once.

ice cubes. Don't use small ones; they will quickly dissolve in a hot atmosphere and dilute the mixture.

Don't serve very fizzy drinks; they are usually extremely sweet and will ruin the flavour of the food that you have so carefully prepared.

At party time, your refrigerator is bound to be filled to capacity with food, leaving you no space to chill the bottles. Simply layer a plastic garbage bin with ice and wine/beer/soft drink bottles or cans to get around this problem. Allow 10 kilos of ice to cool 24 bottles of wine.

Prepare any garnishes ahead of time. If you have your own fruit trees, so much the better. You can slice up lemons, limes and oranges and freeze them well ahead in shallow trays placing freezer wrap between the layers.

If you have more than 20 guests, it is worth paying someone to come and help dispense the drinks and/or food. Or you could enlist the help of a friend or two, or the older children in the family. There are no prizes for making your own life a misery – a great party is one where the host and hostess get to enjoy themselves just as much as the guests!

5

Kebabs and fondue-style nibbles

Fondues are ideal at parties. Place all the items for dipping – crusty French bread, blanched or raw seasonal vegetables, fresh fruit and squares of cake – on a large table to one side of the room. Guests can help themselves. Supply fondue forks or skewers.

Take care that the fondue is kept well stirred to prevent it burning. The fondue mixture can also be placed in a bowl and passed around on a platter for guests to serve themselves.

Bagna Cauda

Preparation time:
  20 minutes
Cooking time:
  10 minutes
Serves 10

1 x 45 g can anchovies, drained and chopped
5 cloves garlic, crushed
100 g unsalted butter
2 egg yolks
selected raw vegetables, cut into 5 cm long sticks

1 Cook the anchovies, garlic and unsalted butter in a medium pan until butter has melted. Transfer mixture to a food-processor bowl. Add egg yolks. Process until mixture is thick.
2 Pour into fondue pot, slowly bring to simmering point. Serve at once with selected vegetables and skewered crusty bread. Fondue may also be served in a bowl and passed around on a platter with the bread and vegetables for guests to help themselves.

Note: This recipe makes only a small amount but because the flavour is fairly strong it should be sufficient for the number of people specified.

Bagna Cauda (top), Cheese Fondue (bottom, recipe page 8).

Tomato and Olive Fondue

Preparation time:
  40 minutes
Cooking time:
  30 minutes
Serves 15-20

1 tablespoon olive oil
1 onion, finely chopped
1 clove garlic, crushed
2 teaspoons dried
  oregano leaves
1 teaspoon ground pepper
1 x 800 g can peeled
  tomatoes, chopped
¾ cup tomato purée
¼ cup finely chopped
  olives
selected vegetable sticks

1 Heat the oil in a medium pan. Cook the onion, garlic, oregano and pepper until onion is soft. Add tomatoes and tomato purée.
2 Bring to the boil, reduce heat, simmer, uncovered, until mixture has reduced by half and thickened.
3 Pour tomato mixture into processor bowl. Process until smooth.
4 Transfer to fondue pot, slowly bring to simmering point. Stir in olives. Serve with selected vegetable sticks and skewered crusty bread. Fondue may also be served in a bowl and passed around on a platter.

Cheese Fondue

Preparation time:
  20 minutes
Cooking time:
  10 minutes
Serves 10-15

2 cups grated mild
  Cheddar cheese
2 cups grated vintage
  Cheddar cheese
1 cup grated Parmesan
  cheese
¼ cup plain flour
2 teaspoons mustard
  powder
2 cups white wine
2 teaspoons Dijon
  mustard
cubes French bread

1 Combine the cheeses, flour and the mustard powder. Pour the wine into the fondue pot, slowly bring to simmering point. Add heaped tablespoonsful of cheese mixture at a time, stirring after each one until it has melted.
2 Continue process until all the cheese has melted and mixture is thick. Stir in Dijon mustard, season with pepper to taste.
3 Stir until fondue is bubbling and smooth. Keep hot over burner. Supply fondue forks or skewers for dipping cubes of French bread.

This can be made in a pan a day ahead. Keep covered in refrigerator. Reheat gently in fondue pot just before serving.

Creamy Bacon and Asparagus Fondue

Preparation time:
  30 minutes
Cooking time:
  20 minutes
Serves 15-20

30 g butter
¼ cup plain flour
1¼ cups milk
1 x 340 g can asparagus
  spears, drained, chopped
2 rashers bacon, finely
  chopped, cooked
ground pepper
seasonal vegetables

1 Melt butter in fondue pot, add flour, mix well. Cook, stirring, for 1 minute. Gradually stir in milk, heat, stirring, until mixture thickens.
2 Stir in asparagus and bacon, season with pepper to taste. Serve with seasonal, lightly blanched vegetables. Fondue may also be served in a bowl and passed around on a platter for your guests to serve themselves.

Creamy Bacon and Asparagus Fondue (top).
Tomato and Olive Fondue (bottom).

Chocolate Fondue

Preparation time:
  30 minutes
Cooking time:
  20 minutes
Serves 12

250 g cream cheese
250 g dark chocolate,
  grated
1 cup thickened cream
30 g unsalted butter
1-2 tablespoons
  chocolate liqueur or
  brandy
fresh seasonal fruits

1 Beat cream cheese
with electric beaters in a
small mixer bowl until
soft and creamy.
2 Transfer cream
cheese to fondue pot,
add chocolate, cream
and butter. Stir over a
low heat until chocolate
has melted and mixture
is smooth. Add liqueur;
mix well.
3 Serve fondue warm
with a selection of fresh
fruit on skewers and
with wafer biscuits.
Fondue may also be
served in a bowl and
passed around on a
platter for your guests
to help themselves.

Note: Add ⅓ cup
grated white chocolate
for additional flavour.

Fruit Kebabs with Spiced Yoghurt Cream

Preparation time:
  40 minutes
Cooking time:
  15 minutes
Makes about 12

1 punnet strawberries,
  hulled
half a small rockmelon,
  peeled and cut in cubes
2 bananas, peeled and
  sliced
2 apples, cut in cubes
24 white grapes
¼ cup orange juice
1 tablespoon honey

Spiced Yoghurt Cream
¾ cup thickened cream,
  whipped
200 g plain yoghurt
2 teaspoons honey
½ teaspoon ground
  nutmeg
¼ teaspoon ground
  cinnamon
½ teaspoon allspice
¼ teaspoon ground
  ginger

1 Thread two or three
pieces of selected fruit
onto skewers until it is
all used.
2 Brush fruit with the
combined orange juice
and honey. Place under
a moderately hot grill,

turning once. Serve the
kebabs warm with
Spiced Yoghurt Cream.
3 To prepare Yoghurt
Cream: Combine all
ingredients in a small
mixing bowl. Mix well.

Note: Fruit is best cut,
skewered and cooked as
close to serving time as
possible. Sprinkle cut
apple and banana with
lemon juice to prevent
them turning brown.

*Clockwise from top left: Chocolate Fondue, Fruit
Kebabs with Spiced Yoghurt, Melon with Ginger Syrup.*

Melon with Ginger Syrup

Preparation time:
   40 minutes
Cooking time:
   Nil
Makes about 25 skewers

1 rockmelon, halved
1 honeydew melon,
   halved
half a small watermelon

Ginger Syrup
1 cup caster sugar
1 cup water
2 tablespoons brandy
2 tablespoons preserved
   ginger syrup or green
   ginger wine

1 Remove seeds from each of the melons. Using a melon baller, scoop the flesh of each melon into balls. Place balls in a large bowl. Cover. Chill well.

2 To prepare Ginger Syrup: Place sugar and water in a small saucepan. Heat gently until sugar has dissolved. Simmer until slightly thickened.
3 Stir in brandy and ginger syrup. Pour over melons. Cover and chill.
4 To serve, skewer one of each type of melon ball onto a bamboo skewer. Repeat until all the fruit is used.

11

Caramel Toffee Fondue

Preparation time:
  30 minutes
Cooking time:
  20 minutes
Serves 12

½ *cup caster sugar*
½ *cup demerara sugar*
½ *cup condensed milk*
2 *teaspoons cornflour*
1 *cup thickened cream*
seasonal fruits

1 Combine sugars in a large pan. Heat gently over a low heat until sugars dissolve. Remove from heat. Combine a small amount of the condensed milk with the cornflour, mixing until smooth.
2 Add the cornflour mixture and cream to the dissolved sugars.
3 Pour in remaining condensed milk, return pan to the heat. A toffee lump should form.
4 Continue stirring over low heat until the lump dissolves. The fondue should be a dark, rich caramel colour. Transfer mixture to fondue pot. Stir often to prevent it burning. Serve immediately with a selection of skewered fresh fruit.
Fondue may also be served in a bowl and passed around on a platter with skewered fruit for guests to serve themselves.

Note: This fondue is also very good as a topping for ice-cream. It will keep for up to three weeks, covered, in the refrigerator. It can simply be reheated and softened gently on the stove or in a microwave just before use.

Caramel Toffee Fondue.

1. *For Caramel Toffee Fondue: Heat the sugars gently in large pan until dissolved.*

2. *Stir cornflour mixture and the cream into the dissolved sugars.*

3. Pour in the remaining condensed milk and stir to combine.

4 Stir continuously over a low heat until the toffee lump dissolves.

Meatballs and Mint Yoghurt

Preparation time:
  40 minutes
Cooking time:
  10 minutes
Makes about 30

500 g minced lamb
2 tablespoons finely
  chopped mint
2 tablespoons finely
  chopped parsley
1 teaspoon ground
  coriander
1 teaspoon ground
  cardamom
1/4 teaspoon ground
  pepper

Mint Yoghurt
1 cup plain yoghurt
2 tablespoons lemon
  juice
2 cloves garlic, crushed
1 tablespoon finely
  chopped mint
1 tablespoon finely
  chopped coriander

1 Thoroughly combine
all ingredients for
meatballs. Shape into
60 small balls. Thread
two balls onto each
skewer. Refrigerate.
2 Cook meatballs
under a preheated
griller for 10 minutes,
turning frequently. Serve
with Mint Yoghurt.
3 To prepare Mint
Yoghurt: Mix all
ingredients in a bowl.
Transfer to serving bowl.

Prawns and Satay Sauce

Preparation time:
  30 minutes
Cooking time:
  3 minutes
Makes 30

30 large green prawns

Satay Sauce
1/2 cup finely chopped
  sultanas
1/2 cup finely chopped
  raisins
1 cup finely chopped
  peanuts
2 tablespoons grated
  fresh ginger
3 cloves garlic, crushed
1 tablespoon chilli sauce
1 cup white vinegar
1/2 cup sugar
5 tablespoons peanut
  butter
5 cups water

1 Peel and devein the
prawns, leaving the tail
on. Set aside.
2 To prepare Satay Sauce:
Place all the ingredients in
a pan. Heat, stirring, until
dissolved. Reduce heat.
Simmer mixture for about
30 minutes, stirring
occasionally.
3 Thread a prawn onto
each skewer. Brush
lightly with satay sauce.
Cook the skewered
prawns under a hot
griller, turning them
frequently, for 2-3
minutes. Serve prawns
with extra satay sauce.

Japanese-style Kebabs

Preparation time:
  20 minutes + overnight
  marinating
Cooking time:
  10 minutes
Makes about 60

1.5 kg chicken thigh
  fillets
1/2 cup sake or white wine
1/2 cup light soy sauce
1/4 cup sweet sherry
2 tablespoons oil
1 teaspoon chopped
  fresh ginger
1 teaspoon sugar
freshly ground pepper
1 bunch spring onions
  cut into 2 cm pieces

1 Cut the chicken into
bite-sized pieces. Combine
all the other ingredients
except spring onions in a
large glass bowl.
2 Add the chicken.
Cover dish and leave to
marinate overnight in the
refrigerator.
3 Thread chicken onto
skewers, alternating
with spring onion. Grill
kebabs for 5-10 minutes
until golden, turning
them frequently.

Meatballs and Mint Yoghurt (top), Prawns and Satay Sauce (centre), Japanese-style Kebabs (bottom).

Eggplant and Capsicum Skewers

Preparation time:
  1 hour + overnight marinating
Cooking time:
  10 minutes
Makes 30

1 large eggplant, cut
  into thin strips
1 large red capsicum,
  cut in half and seeded
1/4 cup shredded
  basil leaves
1/4 cup olive oil
1/4 cup lemon juice
1 teaspoon ground
  pepper
2 cloves garlic, crushed
2 teaspoons brown sugar

1 Sprinkle eggplant strips with salt. Leave to stand for 15 minutes or until soft and pliable. Wash under cold water, squeeze out excess water.
2 Brush capsicum skin with oil. Grill capsicum until skin is black. Wrap in a damp tea-towel until cool. Rub off skin. Cut capsicum into thin strips.
3 Combine basil leaves, oil, lemon juice, pepper, garlic and sugar in a large mixing bowl. Add eggplant and capsicum. Cover and refrigerate overnight. Thread capsicum and eggplant alternately on bamboo skewers. Place under grill. Cook, turning once, until the eggplant is lightly golden. Serve immediately.

Skewered Beef Malaysian-style

Preparation time:
  30 minutes +
  overnight marinating
Cooking time:
  10 minutes
Makes about 60

1.5 kg rump steak
1/2 cup oil
4 onions, finely chopped
4 cloves garlic, crushed
1 tablespoon ground
  coriander
1 tablespoon ground
  cumin
1 tablespoon turmeric
1 tablespoon chilli
  powder
2 teaspoons dried dill
1/2 cup finely chopped
  hazelnuts
1/2 cup soy sauce
1/4 cup lemon juice
1 tablespoon brown
  sugar
1/4 teaspoon freshly
  ground pepper

1 Cut beef into thin strips. Place in a large ceramic or glass bowl.
2 Heat oil in a large pan. Cook the onion, garlic, spices and dill until onion is tender.
3 Add hazelnuts, soy sauce, lemon juice, sugar and pepper. Cook stirring for 1 minute. Pour over meat. Toss meat well to coat it thoroughly with the marinade.
4 Allow to marinate overnight, covered, in the refrigerator.
5 Thread meat onto skewers. Grill for 5-10 minutes; turn frequently.

Left to right: Calamari Twists, Eggplant and Capsicum Skewers, Skewered Beef Malaysian-style.

Calamari Twists

Preparation time:
  20 minutes +
  overnight marinating
Cooking time:
  10 minutes
Makes about 24

2 large calamari hoods

Marinade
2 teaspoons soy sauce
2 tablespoons sherry
1 tablespoon rice
  vinegar
2 teaspoons honey
1/4 teaspoon five spice
  powder
1/2 teaspoon sesame oil
1 clove garlic, crushed

1 Cut the calamari hoods into thin strips lengthways. Combine marinade ingredients in a medium mixing bowl. Add the calamari, cover and refrigerate overnight. Weave calamari strips onto skewers, three or four strips on each until they are all used.
2 Place skewers under a moderately hot grill. Cook through. Serve hot with a rich, tangy mayonnaise.

Note: The size of the calamari will determine how many skewers this recipe will use. Make sure you buy large ones so the strips are long enough to weave.

Bacon Roll-ups

Preparation time:
  35 minutes
Cooking time:
  3 minutes
Makes about 60

2 x 375 g packets pitted
  prunes
350 g whole blanched
  almonds
20 rashers rindless
  bacon cut into 5 cm
  lengths

1 Preheat oven to
moderate 180°C. Roast
almonds until lightly
golden. Cool. Insert an
almond in the centre of
each prune. Roll each
prune in a strip of
bacon. Secure with
small bamboo skewers.
2 Refrigerate roll-ups
until required. Grill
under a moderately hot
grill, turning frequently
until the bacon strips
are crisp.

Tandoori Chicken

Preparation time:
  40 minutes
Cooking time:
  10 minutes
Makes about 60

1.5 kg chicken thigh
  fillets
2 cups plain yoghurt
1/3 cup white wine
  vinegar
1 tablespoon lemon juice
1 tablespoon ground
  sweet paprika
1 tablespoon cayenne
  pepper
1 tablespoon ground
  coriander
1 tablespoon ground
  cumin
6 cloves garlic, crushed
1 tablespoon grated
  fresh ginger
2 bay leaves
3 green capsicum,
  seeded, and cut into
  small cubes

1 Cut chicken into
bite-sized pieces.
Combine all remaining
ingredients except
capsicum in a large
glass or ceramic bowl.
2 Add chicken. Cover.
Allow to marinate in
the refrigerator
overnight.
3 Thread the chicken
pieces onto skewers,
alternating them with
the cubes of capsicum.
Grill for 5-10 minutes,
turning frequently.
Serve immediately.

HINT

Prepare all garnishes
and mixers for your
beverages ahead of
time (keep chilled if
necessary) for ease of
assembly as drinks
are served to guests.
Don't overdo the
garnishes – they are
just one more thing
for people to handle!

Bacon Roll-ups (left). Tandoori Chicken (right).

1. For Bacon Roll-ups: Insert a roasted
almond in centre of each pitted prune.

2. Roll a strip of bacon around each of
the prunes.

3. Hold the strip of bacon in place with a small bamboo skewer.

4. Grill, turning frequently, until the bacon is golden and crisp.

Cold nibbles

When preparing finger food you can allow your imagination to run riot. Spoil guests with platters of mini quiches, muffins and scones, and an array of pâtés and dips. Use blinis and bread as bases for a wealth of toppings, and cherry tomatoes as 'cases' for fillings.

Aim for a variety of colours, textures and flavours – and, of course, portability. All the recipes given here are compact and easy to eat.

Pizza Frittata

Preparation time:
  30 minutes
Cooking time:
  30 minutes
Serves 20

20 g butter
60 g button mushrooms,
  finely chopped
1 small tomato, peeled,
  seeded, finely chopped
1 small red capsicum,
  seeded, finely chopped
1 small onion, finely
  chopped
1 stick cabanossi,
  finely chopped
1 teaspoon dried basil
  leaves
4 eggs

²/₃ cup cream
¹/₄ cup grated Parmesan
cheese

1 Preheat oven to moderate 180°C. Heat butter in a medium pan, add mushrooms, tomato, capsicum, onion, cabanossi and basil. Cook until soft.
2 Combine the eggs, cream and cheese, mix thoroughly. Add the mushroom mixture. Pour into greased 20 cm pie plate, bake for 30 minutes. Cool the frittata to room temperature. Cut in small wedges to serve.

Note: Use chopped ham or salami, if preferred.

Garlic Toast with Salmon Mayonnaise (left, page 22), Pizza Frittata (centre), Grand Marnier Pâté (right, page 22).

Garlic Toast with Salmon Mayonnaise

Preparation time:
 35 minutes
Cooking time:
 Nil
Makes 32

8 slices of bread, crusts
  removed, cut into
  triangles (see Note)
1/3 cup olive oil
2 cloves garlic, crushed
2 tablespoons olive oil,
  extra
1 capsicum, seeded and
  finely chopped
1 onion, finely chopped
1 tomato, peeled,
  seeded and chopped

Salmon Mayonnaise
2 egg yolks
2 cloves garlic,
  crushed
2 teaspoons lemon juice
3/4 cup olive oil
60 g smoked salmon
freshly ground pepper,
  to taste

1 Preheat oven to
moderate 180°C. Brush
both sides of bread with
combined oil and garlic.
Place on a baking tray.
Bake for 10-15 minutes.
Turn halfway through
cooking. Set aside.
2 Heat the extra oil in
a frying pan. Cook the
capsicum, onion and
tomato until tender.

3 To prepare Salmon
Mayonnaise: Whisk the
first three ingredients
together in a small bowl.
Beat oil into mixture
about a teaspoon at a
time, ensuring all oil is
absorbed before adding
more. The mixture will
have the consistency of
thick cream.
4 Transfer mayonnaise
to a food processor.
Add salmon and pepper.
Process until smooth.
5 Serve garlic toasts
topped with a spoonful
of the capsicum mixture
and a dollop of salmon
mayonnaise.

Note: Alternatively, use
a sliced, crusty French
stick for this recipe.

Grand Marnier Pâté

Preparation time:
 30 minutes
Cooking time:
 Nil
Serves about 15

90 g butter
1 onion, chopped
1 clove garlic, crushed
250 g duck livers,
  trimmed (see Note)
2 tablespoons orange
  juice
1 tablespoon Grand
  Marnier (see Note)
1 tablespoon sour cream
freshly ground pepper,
  to taste

Topping
2 orange slices
fresh chives or parsley
1 1/2 teaspoons gelatine
1/2 cup hot chicken stock

1 Melt butter in a pan.
Cook onion and garlic
until onion is tender.
2 Add livers. Cook for
5-10 minutes. Spoon
the mixture into a food
processor or blender
with all remaining
ingredients. Process
until smooth. Set aside.
3 To prepare Topping:
Arrange the orange
slices (cut into quarters
if you wish), and herbs
in the base of a 2-cup
capacity serving dish.
Sprinkle gelatine over
stock, whisk vigorously
with a fork to dissolve.
4 Pour gelatine mixture
over the oranges to a
depth of 1 cm.
Refrigerate until set.
5 Spoon pâté over the
gelatine layer. Tap gently
and smooth the top.
Refrigerate until set.
Unmould onto a serving
plate. Serve with crackers
or Melba toast.

Note: Chicken livers
may be used in place of
duck livers. Use a
liqueur of your choice
or port in place of the
Grand Marnier, if
preferred. Pâté can also
be made successfully
without the gelatine
topping and served on
cracker biscuits.

Cream Cheese Log

Preparation time:
  20 minutes
Cooking time:
  Nil
Serves about 10

250 g cream cheese
1 cup grated Cheddar
  cheese
4 spring onions,
  finely chopped
¼ cup chopped stuffed
  olives
¼ cup pine nuts,
  toasted
1 gherkin, chopped
1 teaspoon lemon juice
few drops Tabasco sauce
cayenne and ground
  pepper, to taste
⅓ cup finely chopped
  parsley

1 Beat the cream cheese in a bowl until it is smooth. Fold in all the remaining ingredients except for the parsley.
2 Form mixture into a log shape. Roll the log in the chopped parsley to completely cover. Wrap in plastic wrap. Refrigerate log until required. Serve with cracker biscuits.

Note: Cheese log can be made a day in advance. Use different nuts and herbs of your choice.

Cream Cheese Log.

Chicken and Mushroom Pâté

Preparation time:
  30 minutes + several
  hours refrigeration
Cooking time:
  Nil
Serves about 20

250 g chicken livers
1 cup chopped
  mushrooms
1 onion, chopped
1 clove garlic,
  crushed
125 g butter, melted
2 tablespoons brandy,
  (see Note)
2 tablespoons cream
1/3 cup shelled
  pistachio nuts

1 Trim chicken livers, discarding any dark spots or membranes. Chop roughly. Cook liver, mushrooms, onion and garlic in half the butter until the liver is cooked. Cool.
2 Process mixture in a food processor or blender until smooth. This may need to be done in batches. Stir in remaining butter, brandy, cream and nuts.
3 Pour mixture into a serving bowl. Cover with plastic wrap, placing it directly on the surface of the pâté. Refrigerate for several hours or overnight. Serve the pâté with cracker biscuits or toast.

Note: The brandy is optional. When buying brandy for cooking purposes, look for less expensive brands. Port or sherry can be used if preferred. Pâté can be prepared up to two days in advance.

Caviar Eggs

Preparation time:
  20 minutes
Cooking time:
  Nil
Makes 40

20 hard-boiled eggs
1 tablespoon curry
  powder
1 1/2 cups mayonnaise
1 x 45 g jar red caviar
1 x 45 g jar black caviar

1 Halve the eggs lengthways. Remove yolks and push them through a fine sieve into a bowl.
2 Blend in the curry powder and mayonnaise until mixture is smooth.
3 Place filling in a piping bag fitted with a star nozzle. Pipe the mixture into each egg cavity.
4 Garnish with red and black caviar just before serving.

Note: The eggs can be prepared to garnish stage several hours in advance. Cover. Refrigerate.

Chicken and Mushroom Pâté.

Salmon Pâté (left). Caviar Eggs (right).

Salmon Pâté

Preparation time:
  20 minutes + several
  hours refrigeration
Cooking time:
  Nil
Serves about 15

1 x 210 g can salmon
  (see Note)
1 x 200 g tub soft
  cream cheese
1 onion, roughly
  chopped
2 gherkins
2 tablespoons cream
1 tablespoon lemon
  juice
1 teaspoon wholegrain
  mustard
few drops Tabasco sauce
freshly ground pepper,
  to taste

1 Place all ingredients
in a food processor.
Process until smooth.

2 Spoon mixture into a
serving dish. Refrigerate
for several hours before
serving. Serve with
crackers or Melba toast.

Note: Pink or red
salmon may be used in
this recipe, or, if you are
feeling extravagant, buy
200 g smoked salmon
(or off-cuts which can
work out as the cheaper
option) and substitute
for the canned variety.

Blinis with Salami and Aioli.

Blinis with Salami and Aioli

Preparation time:
  40 minutes + 1 hour
  standing
Cooking time:
  Nil
Makes about 25

Blinis
1 cup wholemeal plain
  flour
½ teaspoon cream of
  tartar
½ teaspoon
  bicarbonate of soda
1 egg, beaten
1 cup milk
30 g butter, melted
30 g butter, extra

Aioli
2 egg yolks
2 cloves garlic,
  crushed
2 tablespoons lemon
  juice
½ cup olive oil
freshly ground
  pepper
24 slices salami (see
  Note)

1 To prepare the Blinis: Place flour, cream of tartar and bicarbonate of soda in a bowl. Whisk egg, milk and melted butter together. Make a well in the centre of the dry ingredients. Gradually stir in the egg mixture until smooth. Cover. Stand for 1 hour.

2 Grease base of heavy-based pan with a little of the extra butter. Allow 2 teaspoons of mixture for each blini, cooking four or five at a time. Cook until bubbles appear on surface. Turn to brown other side. Cool on wire rack. Repeat until all mixture is used. Set blinis aside.

3 To prepare Aioli: Place the egg yolks, crushed garlic and lemon juice in a food processor. With the motor running, slowly add the oil in a thin stream until the mixture is thick and smooth. Season to taste with the freshly ground black pepper.

4 To assemble, place a slice of salami on each blini. Spoon the Aioli on top of each. Garnish each blini with a sprinkle of chopped basil or parsley, if desired.

Note: Look for salami which is about 3 cm in diameter to fit easily and neatly on the blinis. Larger slices can be cut to fit. Salamis vary from mild to very hot. For unsuspecting palates, it might be best to err on the side of moderation. Blinis and aioli can both be made several hours in advance. Keep covered.

Pesto-topped Cherry Tomatoes

Preparation time:
  35 minutes
Cooking time:
  Nil
Makes about 50

1 cup chopped fresh
  parsley, firmly packed
2 cloves garlic
2 tablespoons pine nuts
1/4 cup olive oil
2/3 cup grated Parmesan
  cheese
1/4 cup fresh basil leaves
15 g butter at room
  temperature
freshly ground pepper,
  to taste
2 x 250 g punnets
  cherry tomatoes

1 Place the parsley, garlic, pine nuts and oil in a food processor or blender. Purée.
2 Add the remaining ingredients except the tomatoes. Process until well combined.
3 Slice the tops from the tomatoes (see Note). Spoon a little mound of the pesto mixture onto the top of each cherry tomato. Refrigerate until required.

Note: A small amount of tomato flesh may be scooped out of each tomato to allow for a more generous amount of pesto filling to be used. These can be made up to two hours in advance. Jars of pesto can be purchased from delicatessens.

Liverwurst Cottage Dip.

Liverwurst Cottage Dip

Preparation time:
  10 minutes
Cooking time:
  Nil
Serves about 10

1 x 250 g tub cottage
  cheese
125 g liverwurst
1/2 cup mayonnaise
2 dill cucumbers,
  chopped
1 onion, chopped
1 tablespoon capers,
  optional
1 tablespoon prepared
  mustard

1 Place all ingredients in a food processor or blender. Process until mixture is smooth.
2 Transfer to a serving dish. Cover. Refrigerate until required. Serve dip with crackers and corn chips.

Note: Dip can be made a day in advance. Cover and refrigerate.

Greek Cheese and Olive Spread

Preparation time:
  30 minutes +
  overnight refrigeration
Cooking time:
  Nil
Serves about 15

1 cup fresh basil leaves
200 g feta cheese (see
  Note)
155 g butter at room
  temperature
1/2 cup cream
1/3 cup freshly grated
  Parmesan cheese
1 tablespoon drained
  capers
1/4 cup slivered black
  olives
1/2 cup pine nuts, toasted

1 Wash and dry basil;
remove leaves from
stems and coarsely chop.
2 In a food processor
(or by hand) blend
basil, feta cheese, butter,
cream, Parmesan,
capers, olives and all
but 1 tablespoon of the
pine nuts.
3 Transfer to serving
bowl; sprinkle with the
remaining pine nuts.
Cover; refrigerate
overnight. Serve from
the bowl with raw or
blanched vegetables, or
crisp biscuits.

Note: If a less salty mix
is desired, use ricotta
cheese in place of the

feta, adding a squeeze
of lemon juice to taste.
If you are blending the
ingredients for the
spread by hand, ensure
they are all chopped as
finely as possible.

Curried Apple and Onion Quiches

Preparation time:
  30 minutes + 30
  minutes refrigeration
Cooking time:
  15 minutes
Makes 24

2 cups plain flour
200 g butter
2 tablespoons milk

Filling
2 teaspoons oil
1 onion, thinly sliced
1 green apple, peeled
  and grated
1/2 teaspoon curry
  powder
1 cup milk
2 eggs, lightly beaten
1/3 cup cream
1/3 cup grated Cheddar
  cheese

1 Place the flour, butter
and milk in a
food-processor bowl.
Process until mixture
begins to form a ball.
Remove and knead
lightly until smooth.

2 Divide the pastry in
half. Roll out pastry to
3 mm thickness. Cut
out pastry rounds with
an 8 cm cutter. Ease
pastry rounds into
greased, shallow patty
tins. Repeat with other
pastry half. Refrigerate
for 30 minutes.
3 Preheat oven to
moderate 180°C. Heat
the oil in a pan. Lightly
brown the onion; add
the apple and curry
powder, cook, stirring,
for 1 minute. Cool
mixture slightly.
4 Place heaped
teaspoonsful of onion
mixture into each
pastry case. Combine
milk, eggs and cream in
a large jug; mix well.
Pour a small amount of
milk mixture into each
pastry case, just enough
to cover the onion
mixture.
5 Sprinkle with the
grated cheese. Bake for
15 minutes or until
golden. Stand quiches
in their tins until cool.
Remove. Serve warm
or cold.

Note: Quiches are best
assembled and baked
close to serving time.
Pastry can be made,
rolled and placed in
patty tins up to 4 hours
in advance. Refrigerate.

*Clockwise from top: Greek Cheese and Olive
Spread, Pesto-topped Cherry Tomatoes (page 27),
Curried Apple and Onion Quiches.*

1. For Spinach Sushi Rolls: Gradually stir vinegar, sugar and salt into the rice.

2. Pour boiling water over the spinach leaves to cover.

Spinach Sushi Rolls

Preparation time:
 45 minutes
Cooking time:
 Nil
Makes about 20

1 cup short-grain white
 rice
2 cups water
2 tablespoons rice
 vinegar (see Note)
1 tablespoon sugar
1 teaspoon salt
15 spinach leaves
4 teaspoons wasabi (see
 Note)
250 g cooked prawns,
 meat finely chopped,
 or 125 g sushi tuna
 cut into wafer-thin
 slices (see Note)
¼ cup pickled ginger

1 Wash rice well with cold water and drain well. Add rice and water to pan, bring to the boil, reduce heat and simmer, uncovered, until water is absorbed. Cover, reduce heat to lowest possible setting and cook 4-5 minutes. Leave to cool. Gradually stir in the combined rice vinegar, sugar and salt.
2 Place spinach leaves in a bowl. Pour boiling water over to cover. Stand for 30 seconds. Strain. Layer half the spinach on a tea-towel. Overlap to form a base 20 x 30 cm. Place half the rice on top of spinach. Moisten hands with a little vinegar. Spread rice to cover spinach, leaving a 2.5 cm strip uncovered at the top.
3 Spread half of wasabi in a line 2.5 cm from bottom. Top with prawn meat and ginger.
4 Roll up firmly from bottom, in the tea-towel, as for a Swiss roll. Refrigerate for 30 minutes. Remove from towel. Cut into 2.5 cm pieces with a sharp knife. Allow to reach room temperature before serving. Repeat with remaining ingredients. Serve with dipping sauce of light soy sauce and grated ginger.

Note: Rice vinegar has a light, delicate flavour that is very different from Western white vinegar. It is available from health-food shops. Wasabi is similar to horseradish cream, but it is a pale green and the flavour is much hotter. Take care to use only the amount specified. It is available in paste or powdered form from health-food shops. Any type of fresh, raw fish may be used for sushi. Or use cooked crab meat in place of the prawns.

Spinach Sushi Rolls.

3. Top the rice with chopped prawn meat and the pickled ginger.

4. Roll up firmly from the bottom, in the tea-towel, as for a Swiss roll.

31

Tzatziki

Preparation time:
  20 minutes
Cooking time:
  Nil
Serves about 10

2 x 200 g carton
  plain yoghurt
1 cup grated Lebanese
  cucumber, drained
4 cloves garlic, crushed
2 teaspoons white wine
  vinegar
cayenne pepper,
  to taste

Combine all the
ingredients. Refrigerate
until ready to serve.
Serve the dip with crisp
vegetable sticks.

Taramasalata

Preparation time:
  20 minutes + several
  hours refrigeration
Cooking time:
  Nil
Serves about 10

2 x 200 g carton
  plain yoghurt
60 g tarama (see Note)
2 slices wholegrain
  bread, torn, crusts
  removed
2 cloves garlic, crushed
2 teaspoons lemon juice

*freshly ground black
  pepper, to taste*

Combine all the
ingredients in a food
processor. Process until
smooth. Refrigerate
several hours or
overnight. Serve with
crisp vegetable sticks or
with crusty bread.

Note: Tarama (smoked
cod's roe) is available
from most delicatessens.

Guacamole

Preparation time:
  20 minutes
Cooking time:
  Nil
Serves about 10

1 x 200 g carton
  plain yoghurt
1 avocado, peeled and
  stone removed
1 onion, roughly
  chopped
1 clove garlic, crushed
1 tablespoon lemon
  juice
2 teaspoons chilli sauce
few drops Tabasco sauce
freshly ground pepper,
  to taste

Blend all the ingredients
in a food processor
or blender until
smooth. Chill. Serve
with toasted corn chips.

*Clockwise from top: Tzatziki,
Guacamole, Taramasalata.*

Cheesy Cornmeal Muffins

Preparation time:
  30 minutes
Cooking time:
  10 minutes
Makes 36

1½ cups cornmeal
½ cup self-raising flour,
  sifted
½ teaspoon bicarbonate
  of soda, sifted
1 egg, lightly beaten
200 g plain yoghurt
1½ cups milk
½ cup grated Cheddar
  cheese
¼ cup grated Parmesan
  cheese
½ cup mozzarella
  cheese
3 spring onions, finely
  chopped
½ red capsicum, finely
  chopped
½ green capsicum,
  finely chopped
2 rashers bacon, finely
  chopped

1 Preheat oven to hot 200°C. Combine cornmeal, flour and bicarbonate of soda in a large mixing bowl. Combine egg, yoghurt and milk, mix well. Pour into the cornmeal mixture, mix quickly and evenly until smooth. Transfer the mixture to a jug.
2 Combine cheeses, spring onions, capsicum and bacon, mix well.
3 Pour the cornmeal mixture into greased, deep patty tins until tins are two-thirds full. Top with level teaspoonsful of cheese mixture. Bake for 10 minutes. Cool slightly; remove the muffins from the tins while still warm and serve them immediately.

Lavosh Crisps with Smoky Capsicum Dip

Preparation time:
  40 minutes
Cooking time:
  15 minutes
Serves 10-15

4 sheets lavosh bread
  (see Note)
100 g butter, melted
1 small jar lemon
  pepper seasoning

Smoky Capsicum Dip
4 rashers bacon, finely
  chopped
1 red capsicum, finely
  chopped
1 onion, finely chopped
250 g cream cheese,
  chopped

1 Preheat oven to moderate 180°C. Brush each sheet of lavosh bread with melted butter. Sprinkle with lemon pepper seasoning. Cut each sheet into 20 pieces (4 x 5 cm). Cut each piece into halves to make triangles. Place triangles on baking tray. Cook in preheated oven for 5 minutes or until crisp. Remove and cool.
2 To prepare Smoky Capsicum Dip: In a large pan, cook bacon, capsicum and onion until soft and beginning to brown. Place mixture in a food-processor bowl with cream cheese. Process until smooth. Serve with Lavosh Crisps.

Note: Lavosh bread can be found in most supermarkets in the bakery section. Lavosh crisps can be baked and stored in an airtight container up to two days ahead. Dip can be made one day in advance. Store, covered, in refrigerator. Serve at room temperature.

Pistachio and Orange Biscuits

Preparation time:
  50 minutes
Cooking time:
  20 minutes
Makes about 54

1 cup plain flour
½ cup ground
  pistachios
125 g unsalted butter,
  chopped

Pistachio and Orange Biscuits (left), Cheesy Cornmeal Muffins (centre), Lavosh Crisps with Smoky Capsicum Dip (right).

Orange Cream

1/2 cup orange juice
2 teaspoons honey
1 tablespoon brown
  sugar
30 g unsalted butter
125 g cream cheese

1 Preheat oven to moderate 180°C. Place the flour, pistachios and butter in food-processor bowl. Process until mixture comes together. Remove, knead lightly until the mixture has formed a smooth ball.
2 Roll out pastry between two sheets of baking paper. Cut out biscuits with 3 cm round or star-shaped cutter. Bake 10 minutes. Leave on tray to cool.
3 When biscuits have cooled, use a small 2 cm piping bag and pipe on Orange Cream. If a piping bag and nozzle are not available, spoon level teaspoonsful of mixture onto each of the biscuits.
4 To prepare Orange Cream: Combine orange juice, honey, sugar and butter in a small pan. Stir until sugar has dissolved. Reduce heat, simmer, uncovered, until liquid has reduced by half. Remove from heat. Beat cream cheese in a small mixer bowl with electric beaters until it is soft and creamy. Add the orange syrup and mix well.

35

Spinach and Lamb Rolls with Tahini Yoghurt

Preparation time:
  1 hour
Cooking time:
  10 minutes
Makes 60

2 bunches spinach
500 g lamb mince
³/₄ cup chopped prunes
¹/₃ cup pine nuts,
  toasted
2 tablespoons lemon
  juice
¹/₂ teaspoon ground
  cinnamon
¹/₂ teaspoon ground
  cloves
1 teaspoon dried mint

Tahini Yoghurt
200 g plain yoghurt
1 tablespoon tahini (see
  Note)
2 teaspoons honey
1 clove garlic,
  crushed

1 Wash spinach leaves and discard the stalks. Plunge leaves into a pan of boiling water to blanch them. Then plunge into a bowl of iced water (this helps to retain the colour). Remove and pat dry with absorbent paper.
2 Cook mince in a large pan until brown, using a fork as it is cooking to break up any lumps. Add the remaining ingredients; mix well. Remove pan from heat.
3 Place heaped teaspoonsful of mixture on individual spinach leaves. Fold in edges and roll up (if leaves are small, use two to make one roll). Serve rolls cold with Tahini Yoghurt.
4 To prepare Tahini Yoghurt: Combine all ingredients in a small bowl and mix well. Chill until serving time.

Note: Spinach rolls can be filled and rolled up to one day in advance. Store on a baking tray covered with absorbent paper and then cling film in the refrigerator. Tahini Yoghurt can also be made a day in advance. If tahini is not available, you can use 1 tablespoon smooth peanut butter. Tahini can be purchased in jars at delicatessens. Pork or beef mince can be used in place of lamb.

> **HINT**
> To prepare Melba Toast, remove crusts from an unsliced white loaf of bread. Cut in half diagonally. Cut in wafer-thin slices. Place triangles on ungreased oven trays. Bake at 150°C for 30 minutes, or until crisp and golden.

Spinach and Lamb Rolls with Tahini Yoghurt.

1. *For Spinach and Lamb Rolls: Remove spinach leaves from iced water. Pat dry.*

2. *Add prunes, pine nuts, juice, spices and herbs to the cooked mince.*

3. Roll heaped teaspoonsful of the mince mixture in the spinach leaves.

4. For Tahini Yoghurt: Place all the ingredients in a bowl and combine.

Chicken Fruit Rolls

Preparation time:
1 hour
Cooking time:
20 minutes
Makes about 60

8 chicken breast fillets
½ cup finely chopped
  dried apricots
¼ cup water
⅓ cup chopped prunes
⅓ cup cottage cheese
1 x 45 g packet French
  onion soup mix
4 thin slices of ham, cut
  in half

Glaze
20 g butter, melted
2 tablespoons apricot
  jam, melted

1 Preheat oven to
moderate 180°C. Line
two baking trays with
foil; grease foil. Place
chicken fillets between
sheets of cling wrap.
Flatten lightly and
evenly with a rolling
pin. Remove cling wrap.
2 Place apricots and
water in a small pan.
Cook until apricots
have absorbed all the
water and are plump.
Remove from heat.
Beat with a wooden
spoon until mixture is
spreadable. Cool.
3 Place prunes and
cottage cheese in a
food-processor bowl.
Process until smooth.

4 Place fillets skin-side
down and sprinkle each
one with soup mix. Place
a piece of ham on each.
Spread four chicken
fillets with apricot
mixture and the others
with prune mixture.
5 Roll up lengthways,
secure with string or
toothpicks. Place rolls
on baking trays.
6 To prepare Glaze:
Combine melted jam
and butter. Brush glaze
mixture on rolls. Bake
for 20 minutes. Cool.
Slice into rounds, serve.

Pesto and Tomato Toasts

Preparation time:
15 minutes
Cooking time:
5 minutes
Makes about 30

3 flat, white bread rolls,
  thinly sliced
6 large sun-dried
  tomatoes, cut into thin
  strips
150 g fresh Parmesan
  cheese, thinly sliced

Pesto
1 cup packed basil
  leaves
½ cup pecans
¼ cup olive oil
3 garlic cloves

1 Toast the bread
slices under grill until
browned on both sides.

2 Spread pesto mixture
evenly over toasted
bread. Top each slice
with sun-dried tomatoes
and Parmesan cheese.
3 To prepare Pesto:
Place the basil leaves,
pecans, oil and garlic in
a food-processor bowl.
Process until mixture is
well combined.

Corn Fritters with Chive Cream

Preparation time:
40 minutes
Cooking time:
20 minutes
Makes about 100

1 cup self-raising flour
2 eggs, lightly beaten
1 x 310 g can creamed
  corn
½ cup milk

Chive Cream
125 g cream cheese
1 tablespoon sour cream
1 tablespoon
  mayonnaise
2 tablespoons chopped
  chives

1 Sift flour into a large
mixing bowl, make a
well in the centre. Blend
in eggs, corn and milk,
mix well. Let mixture
stand for 10 minutes.
2 Heat a large, shallow
pan, brush with melted
butter or oil. Drop two
teaspoonsful of mixture
into the pan in batches.

*Pesto and Tomato Toasts (top), Corn Fritters
with Chive Cream (centre), Chicken Fruit Rolls (bottom).*

When bubbles appear
on the surface, turn and
cook other side. Place
cooked fritters on plate.
Place some of the Chive

Cream onto each of the
fritters to serve.
3 To prepare the Chive
Cream: Beat the cream
cheese in a small mixer

bowl with electric
beaters until it is soft
and creamy. Add all the
remaining ingredients,
mix thoroughly.

39

Asparagus Hollandaise Rolls

Preparation time:
  30 minutes
Cooking time:
  15 minutes
Makes about 30

1 bunch fresh asparagus
30 slices fresh white
  bread

Hollandaise Sauce
1 tablespoon white
  vinegar
½ teaspoon dried
  tarragon
5 peppercorns

2 egg yolks
125 g unsalted butter,
  melted
2 teaspoons lemon juice

1 Cut asparagus spears
in half. Place in medium
pan with a small amount
of water. Cook over a
low heat until just tender.

Asparagus Hollandaise Rolls (top), Salmon and Cucumber Rounds (left),
Caraway Scones with Fruity Butter (right).

Plunge into cold water, drain. Pat dry with absorbent paper.

2 Cut a round from each bread slice with an 8 cm cutter.

3 Place a piece of asparagus across each of the bread rounds. Spoon a teaspoonful of Hollandaise Sauce on top. Fold in half, secure edges with a toothpick.

4 To make Hollandaise Sauce: Combine vinegar, tarragon and peppercorns in a small pan. Heat, reduce liquid to 1 teaspoon. Place egg yolks in a food-processor bowl. Add strained vinegar reduction. Process. Add melted butter in a thin, steady stream through the chute in the processor lid while the machine is still in motion. Process until mixture is thick; add lemon juice.

Caraway Scones with Fruity Butter

Preparation time:
  30 minutes
Cooking time:
  15 minutes
Makes about 16

2 cups self-raising flour
50 g butter, chopped
3/4 cup buttermilk
*2 teaspoons caraway
  seeds*

Fruity Butter
100 g unsalted butter
2 teaspoons fruit chutney

1 Preheat oven to hot 200°C. Place flour, butter, buttermilk and caraway seeds in a food-processor bowl. Process until mixture forms a soft ball of dough. Remove; knead lightly on floured surface.

2 Roll out dough to 2 cm thickness. Cut out scones using a floured 4 cm cutter. Place scones close together on a greased baking tray. Brush tops with milk.

3 Bake for 15 minutes. Cool. Break apart and serve with Fruity Butter.

4 To make Fruity Butter: Beat butter in a small bowl with electric beaters until light and creamy, add chutney, mix well to combine.

Note: Caraway seeds can be replaced with onion flakes or a variety of other seeds or herbs. Any kind of chutney is suitable for this recipe.

Scones can be made up to a day in advance and stored in an airtight container. Reheat by covering with foil and placing in a moderate oven 180°C for about 8 minutes. Use a 2 or 3 cm cutter for making smaller scones.

Fruity Butter can be made up to two days in advance. Wrap and store in the refrigerator. Bring the butter to room temperature to serve.

Salmon and Cucumber Rounds

Preparation time:
  20 minutes
Cooking time:
  Nil
Makes about 40

250 g cream cheese
*1 x 210 g can red
  salmon, drained*
*2 tablespoons finely
  chopped coriander*
1 tablespoon sour cream
2 teaspoons lemon juice
*1 tablespoon finely
  chopped chives*
*1 tablespoon plain
  yoghurt*
ground pepper, to taste
*4 medium Lebanese
  cucumbers*

1 Beat cream cheese in a small bowl with electric beaters until soft and creamy. Add remaining ingredients except the cucumbers and mix well.

2 Slice each cucumber into 10 x 2 cm thick diagonal slices or rounds.

3 Spoon heaped teaspoonsful of the cheese mixture onto the cucumber slices.

Hot nibbles

Always serve a few hot items alongside the cold. If you are well prepared, you'll have no problem fitting in the last-minute work that they require. Some such as Cheese Puffs with Chilli Sauce will need to be cooked just prior to serving; others such as Rosemary Meatballs can be cooked several days ahead and simply reheated on the day.

Provide plenty of napkins so that people can 'cushion' themselves against nibbles that may retain the heat, and also, of course, to contain any juices or sauces that might drip.

Crispy Baked Prawns

Preparation time:
40 minutes
Cooking time:
10 minutes
Serves about 12

24 *medium green prawns, peeled, with tails left on*
2 *eggs*
2 *teaspoons Worcestershire sauce*
2 *teaspoons chilli sauce*
freshly ground pepper
2 *cups grated Cheddar cheese*
1 *cup dry breadcrumbs*

1 Preheat oven to hot 200°C. Butterfly each prawn by cutting it lengthways through the back, nearly all the way through. Remove veins. Flatten prawns slightly.
2 Whisk eggs, sauces and pepper to taste. Dip prawns in egg mixture, then into combined cheese and crumbs. Press on well to coat.
3 Place on a baking tray lined with baking paper. Bake 10 minutes. Serve hot with soy sauce or sweet and sour sauce.

Note: Use 400 g white fish fillets cut into strips in place of the prawns.

From the top: Prawn and Feta Triangles (page 45), Cheese Puffs with Chilli Sauce (page 44), Crispy Baked Prawns, Sesame Chicken Sticks (page 44).

Sesame Chicken Sticks

Preparation time:
  25 minutes +
  overnight marinating
Cooking time:
  25 minutes
Serves about 20

4 *chicken breast fillets,*
  cut into strips
¼ *cup teriyaki sauce*
1 *tablespoon chilli sauce*
1 *tablespoon plain*
  yoghurt
2 *teaspoons curry powder*
2 *cups crushed cornflakes*
¼ *cup sesame seeds*
⅓ *cup grated Parmesan*
  cheese

Sweet and Sour Sauce
1 *cup water*
½ *cup white vinegar*
½ *cup caster sugar*
¼ *cup tomato sauce*
1 *teaspoon chicken*
  stock powder
1 *tablespoon cornflour*

1 Combine the chicken strips in a large bowl with the teriyaki sauce, chilli sauce, yoghurt and curry powder. Mix well. Cover and refrigerate overnight, stirring occasionally.
2 Preheat the oven to moderately hot 190°. Combine remaining ingredients in a shallow dish. Drain the excess marinade from chicken. Coat each chicken strip in the crumb mixture.
3 Place the strips in a single layer on a greased oven tray. Bake for 20-25 minutes or until golden and crisp. Serve hot with Sweet and Sour Sauce.
4 To prepare Sweet and Sour Sauce: Mix all the ingredients in a small saucepan, bring to boil, simmer until thickened.

Note: Crumbed chicken strips can be frozen in a single layer for later use.

Cheese Puffs with Chilli Sauce

Preparation time:
  40 minutes
Cooking time:
  4 minutes each batch
Serves about 12

1 *cup water*
60 *g butter*
1 *cup plain flour, sifted*
4 *eggs*
½ *cup grated pecorino*
  cheese
1 *teaspoon wholegrain*
  mustard
oil for deep-frying

Chilli Sauce
1 *cup water*
2 *cloves garlic,*
  crushed
2 *tablespoons sugar*
2 *tablespoons chilli*
  sauce
3 *teaspoons cornflour*
ground pepper, to taste

1 Place the water and butter in a small pan. Bring to the boil slowly, ensuring that the butter has melted before boiling point is reached. Do not allow to boil.
2 Remove from heat. Add the flour all at once. Return to heat. Beat constantly with a wooden spoon until mixture forms a smooth paste which leaves the sides of pan.
3 Transfer to a large bowl. Cool slightly. Add eggs one at a time, beating well after each addition. The batter should be thick, smooth and shiny. Stir in cheese and mustard.
4 Heat the oil in a saucepan. Drop level tablespoonsful of mixture into the hot oil. Cook for 3-4 minutes until golden brown. Drain the puffs on absorbent paper. Serve with Chilli Sauce.
5 To prepare Chilli Sauce: Combine the water, garlic, sugar and chilli sauce in a small pan. Bring to the boil. Reduce heat.
6 Blend cornflour with a little of the liquid to form a smooth paste. Blend into the chilli mixture. Heat, stirring constantly, until the mixture boils and thickens. Simmer for 3 minutes, season with ground pepper, to taste.

Rice Balls with Cheese

Preparation time:
30 minutes +
30 minutes standing
Cooking time:
3 minutes each batch
Makes about 24

1 small onion, finely
  chopped
15 g butter
2/3 cup short-grain rice
1 cup chicken stock
1/4 cup white wine
2 eggs, lightly beaten
1/4 cup finely chopped
  mushrooms
2 slices ham, finely
  chopped
2 teaspoons finely
  chopped parsley
24 small cubes
  mozzarella cheese
1/4 cup dry packaged
  breadcrumbs
2 tablespoons sesame
  seeds
oil for deep-frying

1 Cook onion in butter until tender. Add rice, stir well to coat with butter. Add combined stock and wine. Bring to the boil, reduce heat, simmer, uncovered, until the liquid has evaporated. Cover. Cook over very low heat until the rice is tender. Cool.
2 Gently stir in the eggs, mushrooms, ham and parsley. Refrigerate mixture for 30 minutes.
3 Using level tablespoonsful of rice mixture, mould the rice around cubes of mozzarella cheese. Roll the rice balls in the combined breadcrumbs and sesame seeds.
4 Deep-fry a few at a time in moderately hot oil until golden brown. Drain on absorbent paper. Serve at once.

Note: Rice balls can be prepared to breadcrumb stage a day ahead.

Prawn and Feta Triangles

Preparation time:
30 minutes
Cooking time:
20 minutes
Makes about 30

5 sheets filo pastry
60 g butter, melted

Filling
125 g feta cheese,
  crumbled
1 cup grated Cheddar
  cheese
4 spring onions, chopped
60 g green prawns,
  peeled, deveined and
  chopped
1 tablespoon chopped
  parsley
1 teaspoon wholegrain
  mustard
1 egg, beaten
black pepper, to taste

1 Working with one sheet of pastry at a time, brush with melted butter. Keep remaining sheets covered with a tea-towel. Cut each of the pastry sheets into six evenly sized strips.
2 To prepare Filling: Combine all ingredients in a small bowl and mix well.
3 Preheat oven to hot 200°C. Place a heaped teaspoonful of the filling on the bottom left-hand corner of one of the pastry strips. Fold the corner over to form a triangle.
4 Continue folding to end of strip, retaining triangle shape with each fold. Brush both sides with butter.
5 Place on a lightly greased baking tray. Repeat the process with the remaining pastry and filling until it is all used. Bake the triangles for 15-20 minutes. Serve hot.

HINT
Cook 20 tiny new potatoes until just tender. Cut a thin slice off the base of each so they stand firmly. Cut an X in the tops, push in sides to form a split. Place on serving tray. Spoon a dollop of sour cream and lumpfish roe on each. Serve warm or chilled.

Savoury Zucchini Boats

Preparation time:
  20 minutes
Cooking time:
  10 minutes
Makes 30

5 large zucchini
1 large tomato, finely chopped
2 spring onions, finely chopped
1 tablespoon chopped parsley
2 slices of salami, finely chopped
1/2 cup grated Cheddar cheese

1 Cut each zucchini into three equal pieces (approx 4 cm). Cut each piece in half lengthways.
2 Using a small teaspoon, scoop a small hollow from each of the slices. Cook the zucchini in simmering water for about 3 minutes, drain. Run under cold water and pat them dry with absorbent paper.
3 Combine all of the remaining ingredients in a small bowl. Spoon the filling evenly into the zucchini boats. Grill the boats until the Cheddar cheese has melted. Serve them immediately.

Spicy Sausage Roll-ups

Preparation time:
  20 minutes
Cooking time:
  20 minutes
Serves about 12

2 sheets frozen shortcrust pastry, thawed
2 tablespoons prepared mustard
5 sticks cabanossi
1 egg yolk, beaten
2 teaspoons cold water

1 Preheat oven to hot 200°C. Cut each pastry sheet in half horizontally. Cut out triangles with a base of 6 cm. Place a small dab of mustard at the base of each pastry piece. Cut the cabanossi into 7 cm lengths and place across mustard on pastry triangles.
2 Dampen the tips of the triangles with a little water. Working from the base, roll each pastry triangle around the pieces of cabanossi. Press lightly to secure tip to rest of pastry.
3 Place the roll-ups on a baking tray. Brush with a mixture of egg yolk and water. Bake for 15-20 minutes or until roll-ups are golden.

Glazed Chicken Wings

Preparation time:
  30 minutes + 1 hour marinating.
Cooking time:
  45 minutes
Serves 20

Spicy Sausage Roll-ups (left), Glazed Chicken Wings (centre), Savoury Zucchini Boats (right).

2 kg chicken wings
1/2 cup bottled barbecue
  sauce
1/2 cup apricot jam
2 tablespoons white
  vinegar
2 tablespoons
  soy sauce
2 tablespoons tomato
  sauce
1 tablespoon sesame oil
2 cloves garlic, crushed

1 Remove wing tips from chicken and trim away excess fat.
2 Stir barbecue sauce, apricot jam, vinegar, soy sauce, tomato sauce, oil and garlic in a small pan over low heat until combined. Pour over chicken wings and mix well. Cover and stand for 1 hour.

3 Preheat oven to moderate 180°C. Drain excess marinade from chicken wings. Place wings in a large baking dish and cook for 45 minutes (you may need to add 1/2 cup water to the dish to prevent wings sticking). Turn wings halfway through the cooking.

Vegetable Fritters

Preparation time:
  30 minutes
Cooking time:
  6 minutes each batch
Serves about 10

1 large potato, peeled
1 carrot, peeled
1 onion
1 zucchini
30 g butter
1/2 teaspoon curry
  powder
2 tablespoons plain
  flour
1 egg, beaten
1/2 cup vegetable oil

Salsa Dipping Sauce
1 tomato, chopped
1 spring onion, sliced
1/4 cup plain yoghurt
2 tablespoons lemon
  juice
1 tablespoon finely
  chopped parsley

1 Coarsely grate each
of the vegetables
separately. Mix potato,
carrot and onion
together. Reserve the
zucchini.
2 Heat butter in pan.
Gently cook the curry
powder for 1 minute.
Add grated potato,
carrot and onion. Cook
for 5 minutes, until the

mixture has thickened
3 Transfer to a bowl.
Add grated zucchini
and flour. Mix well. Stir
in egg until well
combined.
4 Heat oil in frying
pan. Drop level
tablespoonsful of
mixture into pan. Cook
on both sides until
crisp. Drain on
absorbent paper. Serve
with the Salsa Dipping
Sauce.
5 To prepare Salsa
Dipping Sauce: Place all
ingredients in a food
processor or blender.
Process until smooth.

Crab Puffs

Preparation time:
  40 minutes
Cooking time:
  4 minutes each batch
Makes about 12

60 g butter
1/2 cup water
1/2 cup plain flour
2 eggs
1 x 200 g can crab
  meat, drained
1/4 cup finely chopped
  mushrooms
1 teaspoon ground
  ginger
1 tablespoon
  mayonnaise
1 tablespoon slivered
  almonds, toasted
2 teaspoons chopped
  chives
1 1/2 cups vegetable oil

Vegetable Fritters and Salsa Dipping Sauce.

Sauce
1/2 cup teriyaki sauce
2 tablespoons vinegar
1 teaspoon sesame oil

1 Place butter and water in a small pan. Bring to the boil slowly, ensuring butter has melted before boiling point is reached. Do not allow to boil.
2 Remove from heat. Add flour all at once. Return to heat. Beat constantly with a wooden spoon until mixture forms a smooth paste which leaves sides of pan. Cool slightly.
3 Add eggs one at a time, beating well after each addition. The batter should be thick, smooth and shiny. Stir in crab, mushrooms, ginger, mayonnaise, almonds and chives.
4 Heat oil in saucepan. When it is moderately hot, drop in level tablespoonsful of batter mixture. Cook until golden. Remove with a slotted spoon. Drain on absorbent paper. Serve with Sauce.
5 To prepare Sauce: Place all ingredients in a screw-top jar. Shake well until combined.

Note: These puffs are very versatile. The basic recipe can be adapted to include ham, chicken or an ingredient of your choice in place of crab.

Crab Puffs.

Basil Slices

Preparation time:
* 25 minutes*
Cooking time:
* 10 minutes*
Serves about 15

2 French sticks, sliced
* diagonally*
250 g mozzarella
* cheese, sliced*
1 x 45 g can anchovies,
* thinly sliced*
1/4 cup finely chopped
* olives*

Pesto
1 cup chopped
* fresh basil*
2 cloves garlic
1/4 cup toasted pine nuts
1/4 cup olive oil

1 To prepare the Pesto: Place basil, garlic and pine nuts in a food processor or blender. Process until finely chopped. With motor running, gradually pour the oil through chute. Set aside.
2 Spread bread slices with pesto, top with a slice of cheese. Lay the anchovies on top and sprinkle with olives. Grill or bake in a moderate oven until the cheese melts. Serve warm.

HINT
Many types of bread grill or bake well. Try spreading the same topping on two or more varieties.

Beef Samosas

Preparation time:
  30 minutes
Cooking time:
  15 minutes
Makes 45

500 g beef mince
2 teaspoons ground
  cumin
1 teaspoon ground
  coriander
¼ teaspoon turmeric
1 teaspoon curry
  powder
2 teaspoons beef stock
  powder
220 g potato, grated
½ cup water
1 x 375g packet frozen
  ready-rolled shortcrust
  pastry, defrosted

1 Preheat oven to
moderate 180°C. Cook
mince in large pan
until brown, using a
fork to break up any
lumps. Add the spices,
stock powder and
potato. Stir in water,
cook until the potato is
soft. Remove mixture
from heat, cool.
2 Cut the pastry into
rounds with an 8 cm
cutter. Place a level
teaspoonful of the
mince mixture on each
of the rounds.
3 Brush edges with
milk. Fold rounds in
half, press edges together.
Place the samosas on a
greased baking tray.

Brush tops with milk.
Bake for 10-15 minutes
or until lightly golden.
Serve immediately with
mango chutney.

Mushrooms in Beer Batter with Chilli Sauce

Preparation time:
  25 minutes +
  30 minutes standing
Cooking time:
  2 minutes each batch
Serves about 10

1 cup plain flour
pinch salt, optional
1 tablespoon finely
  chopped parsley
30 g butter, melted
¾ cup flat beer
1 egg, separated
oil for deep-frying
350 g button mushrooms

Chilli Sauce
2 cloves garlic, crushed
2 tablespoons chilli
  sauce
1 cup water
2 tablespoons sugar
3 teaspoons cornflour
freshly ground pepper,
  to taste

1 Sift flour and salt
into a bowl. Add
parsley. Mix well.
2 Whisk together
butter, beer and egg

yolk. Make a well in
the centre of the flour.
Gradually add the
liquid, beating
continuously until
smooth. Allow mixture
to stand for 30 minutes.
3 Beat egg white until
stiff peaks form. Fold
lightly into batter.
4 Heat oil in a deep
pan. Dip mushrooms
into batter one at a
time, ensuring they are
totally covered. Drop
into hot oil. Fry for
1-2 minutes, turning if
necessary.
5 Lift out with slotted
spoon. Drain on
absorbent paper. Keep
hot. Repeat with
remaining mushrooms.
6 To prepare Chilli
Sauce: Combine garlic,
chilli, water and sugar
in a small pan. Bring to
the boil. Reduce heat.
Blend cornflour with a
little of the mixture.
Add to pan with freshly
ground pepper, stirring
constantly. Simmer for
3-5 minutes until
slightly thickened. Serve
sauce hot or cold with
the mushrooms as a
delicious entrée or an
hors d'oeuvre.

Note: If you know your
guests like spicy food,
add 2 teaspoons
chopped fresh chilli to
sauce for extra 'heat'.

*Clockwise from top: Mushrooms in Beer Batter,
Beef Samosas, Basil Slices (page 49).*

Spring Rolls

Preparation time:
  35 minutes
Cooking time:
  12 minutes
Serves about 12

1 packet large
  spring-roll wrappers
2 dried Chinese black
  mushrooms, soaked
2 small chicken breasts
2 spring onions, finely
  chopped
100 g bamboo shoots,
  finely chopped
1 red capsicum, chopped
vegetable oil for
  deep-frying
120 g bean sprouts,
  chopped
1 tablespoon dark soy
  sauce
2 teaspoons finely
  grated green ginger
1 tablespoon sweet sherry
1/2 teaspoon sugar

1 Separate wrappers.
Cut each one into four
squares and cover with
a cloth until needed.
2 Squeeze water from
mushrooms, trim away
stems, then shred finely.
Cut the chicken into
small shreds.
3 Cook the chicken,
mushrooms, spring
onion, bamboo shoots
and capsicum in
2 tablespoons of the oil
until the chicken turns
white. Add the bean
sprouts and cook them

briefly. Add soy sauce,
ginger, sherry and the
sugar. Cool.
4 Place 2 teaspoonsful
of filling on each piece
of wrapper and fold
one point over. Fold in
the two side points,
then roll up towards the
last point, forming a log
shape. Dip end in water
to stick wrapper down.
5 Deep-fry spring rolls
in batches in
moderately hot oil until
golden. Drain, serve
with soy or plum sauce.

Note: If the filling is
very moist, use 2 spring
roll wrappers together
to ensure that the
mixture does not seep
during cooking.

Prawn Toast

Preparation time:
  35 minutes
Cooking time:
  15 minutes
Serves about 12

6 slices white bread
250 g green prawns,
  shelled and deveined
1 tablespoon oyster
  sauce
2 teaspoons cornflour
2 teaspoons chopped
  fresh coriander
1/2 teaspoon chopped
  fresh ginger
1 egg, beaten
1 cup sesame seeds
oil for deep-frying

1 Trim the crusts from
bread. Cut each slice
into quarters (triangles)
diagonally. Set aside.
2 Place prawns, oyster
sauce, cornflour,
coriander and ginger in
a food processor or
blender. Process until
smooth.
3 Spread mixture on
one side of each piece
of bread. Brush all over
with egg. Sprinkle with
sesame seeds.
4 Heat oil in deep pan
until surface begins to
move. Deep-fry a few
pieces of bread at a time
until golden brown.
Drain on absorbent
paper. Keep warm.
Continue with
remaining pieces. Serve
with plum sauce.

Dim Sims

Preparation time:
  40 minutes
Cooking time:
  3 minutes each batch
Makes about 60

1 carrot, grated
1 cup finely chopped
  cabbage
3 spring onions,
  chopped
1/4 cup chopped
  bamboo shoots
1/4 cup chopped
  mushrooms
1 x 200 g tin prawns,
  drained
2 tablespoons cornflour

Clockwise from top: Prawn Toast, Steamed Dim Sims, Spring Rolls.

2 teaspoons soy sauce
1 tablespoon vegetable
 oil
1 teaspoon sesame oil
1 egg, beaten
½ teaspoon grated
 fresh ginger
1 x 250 g packet
 prepared wonton
 wrappers

1 Combine the grated carrot, cabbage, spring onion, bamboo shoots, mushrooms and prawns in a large bowl. Whisk the cornflour, soy sauce, oils, egg and grated ginger together in a small bowl. Stir into the vegetable mixture.
2 Remove wrappers from packet. Work with just one at a time, keeping the remainder covered with a damp tea-towel to prevent them from drying out.

3 Place a teaspoonful of mixture towards the tip of one corner of wrapper. Fold the corner over and roll up. Brush with egg to seal. Pinch edges, bring them together and twist.
4 Place in a pan of boiling water. Simmer until just tender, about 3 minutes. Drain. Serve dim sims hot with soy and chilli sauces.

53

Spinach and Feta Bread Cases

Preparation time:
  30 minutes
Cooking time:
  20 minutes
Serves about 20

20 slices wholemeal bread
90 g butter, melted
150 g frozen spinach,
  thawed
150 g feta cheese,
  crumbled
6 eggs, beaten
2 tablespoons milk
¼ teaspoon ground
  nutmeg

1 Preheat oven to moderate 180°C. Trim crusts from bread. Flatten bread slightly, use to line greased muffin tins. Trim excess. Brush well with butter. Bake about 15 minutes, or until crisp and golden.
2 Drain spinach well. Combine with cheese. Place 1 tablespoonful in each bread case.
3 Whisk eggs, milk and nutmeg together. Pour over spinach and cheese to fill cases.
4 Bake for further 5 minutes or until set.

Note: Prepare and bake bread cases without filling two days ahead.

Three Cheese Triangles

Preparation time:
  40 minutes
Cooking time:
  10 minutes
Serves about 20

1 x 375 g packet filo
  pastry
125 g butter, melted
  (see Note)

Three Cheese Filling
2 cups grated Cheddar
  cheese
½ cup grated Parmesan
  cheese
125 g blue vein cheese,
  crumbled
freshly ground pepper

1 Preheat oven to hot 200°C. Unroll the pastry and remove one sheet. Keep remainder covered with a damp tea-towel.
2 Brush sheet with melted butter. Cut into 8 evenly sized strips.
3 To prepare Three Cheese Filling: Combine all the ingredients.
4 Place a teaspoonful of filling on the bottom left-hand corner of each pastry strip. Fold corner over to form a triangle.
5 Continue folding to the end of strip, retaining the triangular shape with

each fold. Brush with melted butter.
6 Place on a lightly greased baking tray. Continue with the remaining pastry and filling.
7 Bake for 10 minutes. Serve hot.

Note: This is only a suggested quantity of butter. You may find you need more. Melt in small quantities to avoid waste. Triangles may be covered with plastic wrap and refrigerated

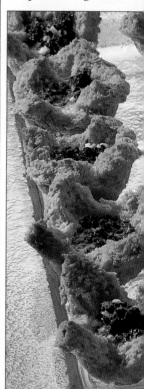

From left to right: Spinach and Feta Bread Cases, Crab-stuffed Mushrooms, Three Cheese Triangles.

overnight. Or, cover them and freeze on trays until required. If frozen, cook for 10 minutes in a hot oven 200°C, then for a further 5-10 minutes in a moderate oven 180°C.

Crab-stuffed Mushrooms

Preparation time:
  25 minutes
Cooking time:
  6 minutes
Makes 24

24 *small cap mushrooms*
30 g *butter*
4 *spring onions,*
  chopped
1 x 200 g *can crab*
  meat, drained
2 *tablespoons lemon*
  juice
½ *teaspoon chilli*
  powder
freshly ground pepper,
  to taste
1 *cup sour cream*
¼ *cup grated Parmesan*
  cheese
1 *cup grated Cheddar*
  cheese
paprika

1 Preheat oven to moderate 180°C. Remove mushroom stalks. Chop finely. Set aside. Place mushroom caps on baking tray.
2 Place butter, spring onions, crab, lemon juice and seasonings in a bowl.
3 Stir in mushroom stalks with sour cream and Parmesan. Spoon even amounts of mixture into caps. Sprinkle with Cheddar and paprika.
4 Cook 5-6 minutes or until heated and cheese melts. Serve at once.

Mushroom or Tuna Puffs

Preparation time:
  30 minutes
Cooking time:
  30 minutes
Makes about 80

1 x 1 kg packet
  ready-rolled puff
  pastry sheets, defrosted
1 egg, beaten

Tuna Filling
1 x 220 g can tuna
2 spring onions
125 g cream cheese
ground pepper, to taste

Mushroom Filling
6 rashers rindless
  bacon, chopped
100 g mushrooms
½ cup grated Parmesan
  cheese
1 egg

1 Preheat oven to very
hot 220°C. Cut out
24 x 4 cm rounds from
pastry using a sharp
cutter.
2 Combine all the
ingredients thoroughly
for desired filling. (If
combining by hand,
chop ingredients very
finely.) Place
½ teaspoonful of the
mixture on the centre of
each round.
3 Brush edges with a
little egg. Fold pastry in
half. Press the edges
together carefully to

seal them. Use a fork to
decorate the edges.
4 Place on a non-stick
baking tray. Brush top
with egg. Bake for
25-30 minutes or until
golden brown. Serve the
mushroom or tuna
puffs hot.

Note: The puffs can be
assembled several hours
ahead of time. Store,
covered, in the
refrigerator. Sesame seeds
may be sprinkled over
the puffs prior to baking.

Pumpkin and Camembert Muffins

Preparation time:
  30 minutes
Cooking time:
  15 minutes
Makes about 25

1 cup cooked, mashed
  pumpkin
20 g butter, melted
1 tablespoon sour cream
2 tablespoons finely
  chopped chives
2 eggs, separated
1 cup self-raising flour
125 g Camembert
  cheese, cut in 1.25 cm
  squares
¼ cup flaked almonds

1 Preheat the oven to
moderate 180°C.
Combine the pumpkin,
butter, sour cream,

chives, egg yolks and
flour in a large mixing
bowl. Mix until smooth.
2 Place egg whites in a
small mixer bowl. Beat
with electric beaters
until soft peaks form.
Using a metal spoon,
fold beaten egg whites
into pumpkin mixture.
3 Place heaped
teaspoonsful of mixture
into a greased
mini-muffin tin. Top
with squares of
Camembert cheese and
flaked almonds. Bake
for 15 minutes.
4 Serve warm, either
plain or spread with
some butter whipped
with chopped chives.

Satay Scrolls

Preparation time:
  20 minutes
Cooking time:
  20 minutes
Makes about 60

1 teaspoon oil
1 onion, finely chopped
1 clove garlic,
  crushed
1 teaspoon turmeric
1 teaspoon ground
  cumin
1 tablespoon sweet
  chilli sauce
½ cup crunchy peanut
  butter
¾ cup coconut milk
1 x 1 kg packet frozen
  ready-rolled puff
  pastry, defrosted

Clockwise from top: Mushroom or Tuna Puffs, Satay Scrolls, Pumpkin and Camembert Muffins.

1 Preheat oven to very hot 220°C. Heat the oil in a medium pan. Add the chopped onion and garlic, cook until soft.
2 Stir in the turmeric, cumin, chilli sauce, crunchy peanut butter and coconut milk. Mix until well combined and thick. Cool the mixture slightly.
3 Lay out the five pastry sheets over the work surface and spread the satay sauce evenly over them.
4 Roll pastry sheets up firmly and evenly. Cut each roll into 12 rounds with a sharp serrated or electric knife. Place the scrolls on greased baking trays. Bake for 10-15 minutes or until they are crispy and golden. Serve at once.

57

Rosemary Meatballs with Red Wine Sauce

Preparation time:
  35 minutes
Cooking time:
  10 minutes
Makes about 45

750 g beef mince
1 egg, lightly beaten
2 cloves garlic, crushed
3 teaspoons freshly
  ground pepper
2 tablespoons tomato
  paste
1 onion, finely chopped
2 tablespoons rosemary,
  finely chopped
1 tablespoon
  Worcestershire sauce
oil for frying

Red Wine Sauce
1½ cups red wine
1 clove garlic, crushed
½ cup tomato purée
½ cup water
2 teaspoons mustard
30 g butter

1 Thoroughly combine all the ingredients for meatballs. Shape level tablespoonsful of mixture into balls.
2 Heat oil in a large, shallow pan. Add meatballs and cook, shaking pan often, (this helps meatballs keep their shape) until mince is cooked and meatballs are evenly browned.

Drain on absorbent paper. Serve with Red Wine Sauce.
3 To prepare Red Wine Sauce: Drain oil from pan. Add the wine and garlic to the pan juices, bring to the boil until liquid is reduced by half. Strain liquid into medium saucepan. Add the tomato purée, water and mustard. Bring to boil, reduce heat, simmer until reduced by half, whisk in butter. Serve sauce warm with the meatballs.

Note: Meatballs and sauce can be cooked several days prior to using. Keep covered in the refrigerator. Reheat in moderate oven 180°C before serving.

Leek and Mushroom Crêpe Rolls

Preparation time:
  45 minutes
Cooking time:
  20 minutes
Makes 25

⅓ cup plain flour
3 eggs, lightly beaten
¾ cup milk
20 g butter
1 leek, thinly sliced

250 g mushrooms, thinly
  sliced
lemon pepper
  seasoning, to taste

1 Sift flour into mixing bowl. Whisk in combined eggs and milk until smooth. Allow to stand for 10 minutes.
2 Heat large, shallow pan. Brush with melted butter or oil. Pour about one fifth of the mixture into the pan. Swirl to spread mixture evenly over base of pan. Cook until lightly golden on underside. Remove from pan; set aside. Repeat process with the remaining mixture until you have five crêpes.
3 Melt butter in small pan, add leek and mushrooms. Cook until soft. Stir in lemon pepper seasoning.
4 Cut each crêpe into five wedges. Place heaped teaspoonsful of mixture onto the narrower end of the wedge. Roll up crêpes. Place on a greased baking tray.
5 Warm in a moderate oven 180°C just before serving.

Note: Crêpes can be made up to two days in advance. Keep covered in the refrigerator.

Rosemary Meatballs (top). Leek and Mushroom Crêpe Rolls (bottom)

Cheesy Mushroom and Oyster Bites

Preparation time:
  20 minutes + 40
  minutes refrigeration
Cooking time:
  10 minutes
Makes about 30

50 g butter
2 tablespoons plain flour
1/2 cup milk

150 g mushrooms,
  chopped
1 x 105 g can smoked
  oysters, chopped
4 spring onions, finely
  chopped
1/3 cup grated Cheddar
  cheese
freshly ground pepper
1 cup plain flour,
  extra
2 eggs, lightly beaten
1 1/2 cups oat bran
oil for deep-frying

1 Melt butter in medium pan. Add flour, cook, stirring, for 1 minute. Remove from heat, gradually stir in milk. Return to heat, stirring continually until mixture thickens.
2 Add the mushrooms, oysters, onions and cheese. Season with freshly ground pepper to taste. Cover mixture and refrigerate until

firm, about 40 minutes.
3 Roll heaped teaspoonsful of mixture into balls. Carefully roll balls in extra flour. Roll in lightly beaten egg and then in the oat bran.
4 Heat the oil in heavy-based, deep pan. Deep-fry balls in moderately hot oil until they are lightly golden. Drain on absorbent paper. Serve bites hot.

Note: Breadcrumbs can be used in place of oat bran. These crunchy bites can be rolled and coated with the oat bran several hours in advance and cooked just before serving. They can also be reheated in a moderate oven 180°C if cold.

Crispy Fish with Dill and Caper Mayonnaise

Preparation time:
  45 minutes
Cooking time:
  20 minutes
Serves about 10

⅓ *cup self-raising flour*
⅓ *cup cornflour*
1 cup milk
2 teaspoons herb pepper
2 egg whites
oil for deep frying
extra flour for coating
400 g white fish fillets,
  cut into thin strips

Dill and Caper Mayonnaise
3 egg yolks
¾ *cup oil*
2 tablespoons lemon
  juice
1 tablespoon chopped
  dill
1 tablespoon chopped
  capers

1 Combine flours in a large mixing bowl. Make a well in the centre, blend in milk and herb pepper.
2 Beat egg whites in a small mixer bowl with electric beaters until soft peaks form. Using a metal spoon, fold the egg whites into the flour mixture to make a batter.
3 Heat oil until moderately hot in a heavy-based pan. Dip fish pieces in extra flour, then into batter, drain excess. Cook fish in oil until lightly golden and crisp.
4 Remove with slotted spoon. Drain on absorbent paper. Serve hot with Mayonnaise.
5 To prepare Dill and Caper Mayonnaise: Place the egg yolks in a food-processor bowl and process. Add oil in a thin stream through the hole in the processor lid while the machine is still in motion. Process until thick, then add lemon juice, dill and capers.

Note: Make mayonnaise up to a day ahead. Fish is best coated and fried just before serving. If short for time, add dill and capers to 1 cup commercial mayonnaise.

Cheesy Mushroom and Oyster Bites (left). Crispy Fish with Dill and Caper Mayonnaise (right).

Mini Pizzas

Preparation time:
 40 minutes
Cooking time:
 10 minutes
Makes about 60

3 cups self-raising flour
75 g butter, chopped
³⁄4 cup buttermilk
¹⁄3 cup milk

Topping
¹⁄2 cup tomato paste
1 tablespoon dried
 oregano leaves
60 g salami, thinly sliced
1 small onion, thinly
 sliced
60 g button
 mushrooms, thinly
 sliced
¹⁄2 avocado
50 g sun-dried
 tomatoes, thinly sliced
¹⁄3 cup sliced olives
150 g Cheddar cheese,
 cut into 2 cm squares

1 Preheat oven to
180°C. Sift flour into
large mixing bowl; add
chopped butter. Using
fingertips, rub butter
into flour until mixture
is a fine, crumbly
texture. Add buttermilk
and milk. Combine
mixture to form a soft
dough.
2 Roll dough out to
5 mm thickness. Cut the
dough into rounds,
using a 6 cm cutter.
Place rounds on greased
baking tray. Combine
the tomato paste and
oregano. Spread tomato
paste evenly over each
of the rounds.
3 Place the topping
combinations on each
round, adding the
cheese last. Bake for
10 minutes. Serve hot.

Note: Any combination
of ingredients can be
used for toppings. Pizza
bases can be rolled and
cut into shape several
hours in advance. Add
the tomato paste and
the chosen toppings just
before baking.

Nutty Pork Rolls with Plum Sauce

Preparation time:
 40 minutes
Cooking time:
 10-15 minutes
Makes 30

500 g pork mince
2 teaspoons grated
 ginger
1 tablespoon soy sauce
2 cloves garlic,
 crushed
1 teaspoon garam
 masala
1 x 375 g packet filo
 pastry
100 g butter, melted
³⁄4 cup ground Brazil
 nuts

Plum Sauce
1 x 825 g can pitted
 plums
¹⁄2 teaspoon sweet chilli
 sauce
1 teaspoon soy sauce
¹⁄4 teaspoon ground
 ginger

1 Preheat oven to
moderate 180°C. Cook
mince in a large pan
until brown, using a
fork to break up any
lumps. Add ginger, soy
sauce, garlic and garam
masala. Mix well.
Remove from heat, cool.
2 Cut filo pastry sheets
in half widthways. Take
a single sheet, brush
lightly with melted
butter, sprinkle with
ground nuts and fold in
half widthways.
3 Place a level
tablespoonful of mince
mixture on one end of
pastry. Fold in edges and
roll up. Repeat with
remaining ingredients.
4 Place rolls on baking
tray. Brush with butter.
Bake for 10-15 minutes
or until lightly golden.
Serve rolls hot with the
plum sauce.
5 To prepare Plum
Sauce: Place all the
ingredients in a
food-processor bowl.
Process until smooth.
Transfer the mixture to
a small pan. Heat
through; serve warm.

Nutty Pork Rolls with Plum Sauce (left).
Mini Pizzas (right).

Index

Flighty

A magical creature Novella

By

HDA Pratt

Books by HDA Pratt

A Magical Creature Series

Flighty
Nerdiver
Nimfa & Master

A Night Creature Trilogy

The Sleepless Night Creature

I dedicate this book to
Joanna Minter
The girl who gave me my reading obsession